JESUS
BE IN ME

Other books by Sarah Hornsby

At the Name of Jesus
Who I Am in Jesus
The Fruit of the Spirit
Getting to Know Jesus from A to Z

JESUS
BE IN ME

SARAH HORNSBY

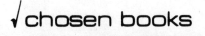

FLEMING H. REVELL COMPANY
TARRYTOWN, NEW YORK

Scripture texts are from the Holy Bible, New International Version, copyright © 1973, 1978, 1984 International Bible Society. Used by permission of Zondervan Bible Publishers.

Library of Congress Cataloging-in-Publication Data
Hornsby, Sarah.
    Jesus be in me / Sarah Hornsby.
       p. cm.
    ISBN 0-8007-9189-4
    1. Lent—Prayer-books and devotions—English.   I. Title.
BV85.H66   1991
242'.34—dc20
                                   91-15197
                                        CIP

A Chosen book
Copyright © 1991 by Sarah Hornsby

Chosen Books Publishing Company, Ltd.
Published by
Fleming H. Revell Company
Tarrytown, New York
Printed in the United States of America

For my daddy
C. E. Anderson
August 3, 1906–October 19, 1990

Acknowledgments

A special thanks to editors Jane Campbell and Ann McMath for encouraging me to try "something different" in the illustrations.

Thanks to Don Ricardo Reyes and other Central American artists who, like early Christian artists, simplified in order to communicate the human story and from whom I have drawn ideas.

Thanks also to artists in Amanecer magazine, Weavings magazine and Jews for Jesus publications; to artists on death row; and others from The Open Door Community newsletter in Atlanta.

Thanks to my family, especially my husband, Jim, for his steady supportiveness; to James for his faithful critiques; to Andy for technical advice; to my mother for her wisdom.

Introduction

As I wrote these pages, meditating on how Jesus can be in me, learning from His experiences as the Suffering Servant and from Moses as the suffering liberator, I had no idea they would speak so directly to my own need. I did not know my daddy was dying of bone cancer when I wrote "Jesus, be in my bones" and "Jesus, be in my dying."

The very day my sister called from South Carolina to tell me to return from Nicaragua because Daddy was very near death, my meditation was on the words of Jesus on the cross, "It is finished." A few days later, just before my sweet daddy died, my meditation was on "Jesus, be in my releasing" and "Father, into Thy hands I commit My spirit."

Then came the resurrection, that certainty of a glorious welcoming, togetherness beyond the pain.

My drawings accompanying these thoughts show a bird with three tailfeathers depicted in many Nicaraguan Indian paintings. When I asked a Nicaraguan artist what the bird stands for, he replied, "The Holy Spirit and peace." As I thought about this bird, I realized that the tailfeathers make a shem, the Hebrew letter meaning "the name," which is understood to refer to God.

I have also depicted a woman with long, black hair. The effect of her eyes and nose is similar to that of early Christian art and actually represents a kind of "Everyperson," since it is a stylized, simplified depiction of woman/man. Although its origin is Nicaraguan, it has a lot with which anyone can identify, especially since the drawings reveal the spectrum of human emotion.For me, then, this book is not just another devotional on already crowded shelves. It is a living witness that God is with us in the midst of our own crucifixion and death. God gives us what we need to minister to others of His reality in the midst of their suffering, and brings us home into Easter joy.

He lives!

Sarah Hornsby
December 1990

JESUS
BE IN ME

Jesus: Born of Mary
Prophecy: Genesis 3:15
Fulfillment: Luke 2:7;
Galatians 4:4–5

Jesus, be in my birth . . .

Every birth is a miracle; each new-
born is marvelously and intricately
made. Father God, You were totally present in Jesus' birth. You
were also present in my birthing
process, both natural and spiritual.
This Lenten Season I want to understand more fully Your reason
for my being born.

Thank You, Father, for my mother. Help me to reflect
Your love and appreciation of her, as Jesus did to
Mary. Forgive her for ways she has caused me pain,
and forgive me for ways I have given her pain. Jesus,
be in my birth . . .

For you created my inmost being; you knit me together in my
mother's womb. I praise you because I am fearfully and wonder-
fully made. . . .   Psalm 139:13–14

Moses: Born of Jochebed
Exodus 6:20

Jesus, be in my children . . .

How wonderful is the birthing process, O Lord, both natural and spiritual. Thank You for the children who have come forth from the womb of my body and the womb of my prayers in Your Spirit. Draw them ever closer to Yourself. They must leave me in order to make their own nests in You, that they may continue the process of birth and nature, establishing their own families. I release them, Lord, one by one into Your hands. In You we are forever united, forever free. Jesus, be in my children . . .

The children of your servants will live in
your presence; their descendants
will be established before you.

Psalm 102:28

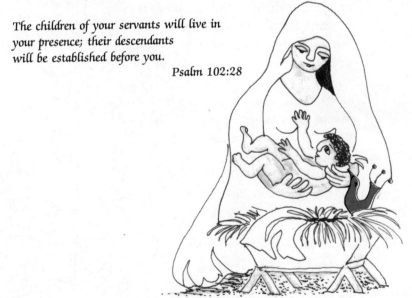

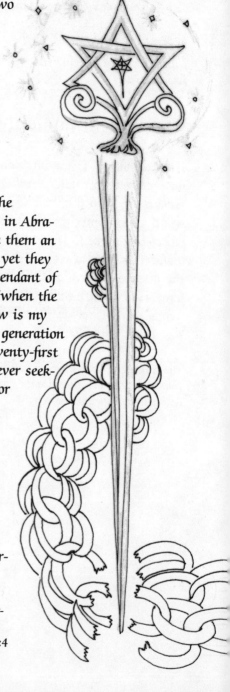

Jesus: Son of Abraham
Prophecy: Genesis 18:18
Fulfillment: Matthew 1:1

Jesus, be in my generation . . .

What a privilege to tell the
story of our ancient roots in Abraham and Sarah! God gave them an
"impossible" assignment, yet they
were obedient. Jesus, descendant of
this tradition, was born "when the
time had fully come." Now is my
time in history, a secular generation
on the threshold of the twenty-first
century. I must be alert, ever seeking more of God's Spirit for
power to fulfill His plan.

God's Word, the Spirit's
Sword, cuts me free from
the rebellion and mistakes
of past generations, so I
can walk free in His will,
fulfilling my appointed
task. Jesus, be in my generation . . .

. . . We will tell the next generation the praiseworthy deeds of
the Lord. . . .   Psalm 78:4

Moses: Son of Abraham
Exodus 2:11, 24–25

Jesus, be in my ancestors . . .

I look back at the way God has worked to bring me to Himself, through the chain of history, the links of my family.

Thank You, Father God of history, for examples of faith, ancestors who went beyond their ability and courage, depending on You for their strength. Jesus, be in my ancestors . . .

He made known his ways to Moses, his deeds to the people of Israel: The Lord is compassionate and gracious, slow to anger, abounding in love. . . . As a father has compassion on his children, so the Lord has compassion on those who fear him; for he knows how we are formed, he remembers that we are dust.

Psalm 103:7–8, 13–14

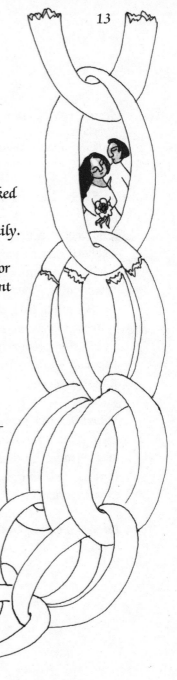

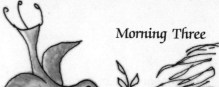

Jesus: Son of Isaac
Prophecy: Genesis 17:19
Fulfillment: Matthew 1:1–2

Jesus, be in my memories . . .

The people of Israel were called by daily liturgy,
Sabbath rest and yearly feasts to remember their
heritage, a family history of failures and faith. I
review all my past, giving every bit to You, righteous Father God, who searches the minds and
hearts of every person. The seal of Your Holy
Spirit stamped with Jesus' sacrificial blood covers
the door to my subconscious, the storage place of
forgotten events.

When a bitter memory comes to consciousness, I
yield it to Your nail-pierced hands, Jesus. Your
sweet fragrance breathes peace, removing the bitterness, teaching me what I need to learn from
that experience. Jesus, be in my memories . . .

For he has not despised or disdained the suffering of the afflicted one . . . but has listened
to his cry for help.   Psalm 22:24

Moses: Son of Isaac
Exodus 2:11, 24

Jesus, be in my foundation . . .

When I came to know that Jesus is the Jewish Messiah God sent to fulfill the prophecies, I became new, born of God's Spirit. After years of doubt, Jesus came to me one spring morning in 1964 as I sat reading the Beatitudes in the tiny dormitory room where we lived when, Jim, my husband, was in his last year of seminary. "If you hunger and thirst for righteousness, justice, you will be filled, satisfied." As I read the companion verses in John, "I am the living water, the living bread," I knew He is alive.

Father God, unshakeable Foundation, through the years I have been discovering the depth of my grounding in You. In Jesus You have set me on a rock and enabled me to build without fear of wind and rain. Jesus, be in my foundation . . .

You are . . . built on the foundation of the apostles and prophets, with Christ Jesus himself as the chief cornerstone . . . being built together to become a dwelling in which God lives by his Spirit.
Ephesians 2:19–22

Jesus: Son of Jacob
Prophecy: Genesis 28:14
Fulfillment: Luke 3:23, 33–34

Jesus, be in my beginnings . . .

How often I begin anew! With every recognition of
specific ways I am deliberately or unconsciously apart
from God's pleasure, I need to ask Him to clean the
slate so I can begin again. In these beginnings I am
reminded of Jacob, who after deceiving his father was
forgiven, given a vision of angels and a promise.

In my struggles I am kin to Jacob, who wrestled with
God. This Lent I bring to You daily, Father God, my
deceptive ways, my struggles, my repentance, to receive
Your cleansing, healing, restoring touch. Jesus, be in
my beginnings . . .

. . . Being confident of this, that he who began a good work in
you will carry it on to completion until the day of Christ Jesus.

                                                        Phillipians 1:6

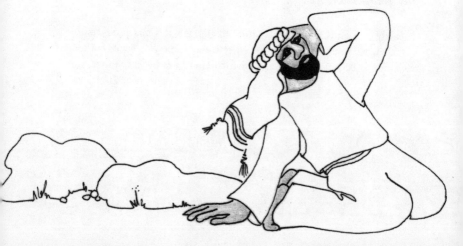

Moses: Son of Jacob
Exodus 2:11, 24

Jesus, be in my establishing . . .

The Spirit of God moved over the formless void to establish the heavens and earth. God is still moving through the chaos of this planet to establish the Lordship of Jesus Christ. I am part of this establishing, and I am not dismayed by seeming setbacks.

Father God, my Strength and Stability, in my weakness, as I join others in fasting and prayer against principalities and powers too great for us, our strength is established. Jesus, be in my establishing . . .

We sent Timothy . . . to strengthen and encourage you in your faith, so that no one would be unsettled by these trials. You know quite well that we were destined for them.

1 Thessalonians 3:2–3

Jesus: Lion of Judah
Prophecy: Genesis 49:10
Fulfillment: Matthew 1:1, 6

Jesus, be in my creation . . .

God worked His plan despite
Joseph's arrogance, his brothers'
jealousy, Israel's favoritism,
Judah's adultery. God planned to
send His pure Son into a people
no different from people today.
Through this tarnished line came
Jesus, the brilliant Messianic Star!

As I read of the gross sinfulness
of the ancestors of Jesus, I am
amazed at God's mercy and pa-
tience. Father God, You can
create good of my past and
turn sin into something
useful. Jesus, be in my
creation . . .

Create in me a pure heart, O
God. . . . Restore to me the joy
of your salvation and grant me
a willing spirit.

Psalm 51:10–12

Moses: Tribe of Levi
Exodus 2:1

Jesus, be in my preparation . . .

Moses had trained, as a son of Egyptian royalty, in warfare and mastery. God's training was slavery, exile, rejection and the obedience school that sent Moses back to Egypt, despite failures and feelings of inadequacy. Persistence in obedience led the people out.

Father God who knows my need, You prepare me to fulfill dreams You implanted even in childhood. Many lessons seem hard, even unnecessary, but as I view the whole, each experience has played its part in making me ready for the road mapped out long ago. Jesus, be in my preparation.

. . . And with your feet fitted with the readiness that comes from the gospel of peace.   Ephesians 6:15

Jesus:
Son of David
Prophecy:
Isaiah 9:6–7; 2 Samuel 7:13
Fulfillment: Luke 2:4–5

Jesus, be in my belonging . . .

Jesus grew up with a real sense of belonging in
the Jewish community. As a son of David, His
heritage was of kings from whom the deliverer
would come. At twelve years of age, Jesus knew
He belonged to His Heavenly Father for a purpose.

My sense of belonging does not have to do
with race, nationality, sex, economic,
marital or educational status, though all
of these can be used to bring God glory.

My belonging stems from my adoption
into the family of faith, making me a
"joint heir with Christ" of all the Spirit
has. Jesus, be in my belonging . . .

The Spirit of the Lord will rest on him—
the Spirit of wisdom and of understanding, the Spirit of counsel and of power,
the Spirit of knowledge and
of the fear of the Lord.
        Isaiah 11:2

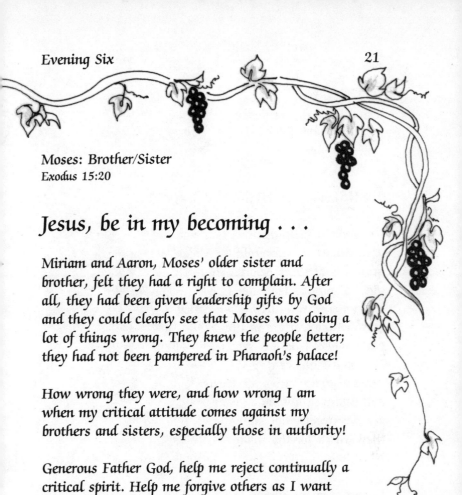

Moses: Brother/Sister
Exodus 15:20

Jesus, be in my becoming . . .

Miriam and Aaron, Moses' older sister and
brother, felt they had a right to complain. After
all, they had been given leadership gifts by God
and they could clearly see that Moses was doing a
lot of things wrong. They knew the people better;
they had not been pampered in Pharaoh's palace!

How wrong they were, and how wrong I am
when my critical attitude comes against my
brothers and sisters, especially those in authority!

Generous Father God, help me reject continually a
critical spirit. Help me forgive others as I want
You to forgive me. Jesus, be in my becoming . . .

Do everything without complaining or arguing, so that you
may become blameless and pure. . . .   Phillipians 2:14–15

Jesus: Babe of Bethlehem
Prophecy: Micah 5:2
Fulfillment: Luke 2:4–5

Jesus, be in my city . . .

Jesus' birth in Bethlehem was no
accident. It was foretold by Micah
hundreds of years before. My birth-
place is no accident, nor is the
city where I now live. I am called
to spiritual warfare in the
place where God has set me.
Fear and violence grip the
heart of many cities, destitute
and depraved humanity wan-
der the streets, not knowing
they search for the living
Jesus.

Father of every human creature, help me make a differ-
ence here where You have
placed me. Jesus, be in my
city . . .

In every city the Holy Spirit warns
me that prison and hardships are
facing me. However, I consider my
life worth nothing to me, if only I
may finish the race and complete
the task the Lord Jesus has given
me.   Acts 20:23–24

Moses: Birth in Egypt
Exodus 2:2

Jesus, be in my citizenship . . .

Since Moses was raised in Pharaoh's palace, he had access to the king when the time came to demand his people's freedom. Paul's Roman citizenship enabled him to witness to governors and rulers about the resurrected Jesus. Our citizenship is no more accidental than our place of residence.

Father God of the nations, show me my responsibility to my earthly homeland as well as my heavenly one. Jesus, be in my citizenship . . .

You are no longer foreigners and aliens, but fellow citizens with God's people and members of God's household.   Ephesians 2:19

Jesus: At the Time Appointed
Prophecy: Daniel 9:25
Fulfillment: Luke 2:1–7

Jesus, be in my time . . .

Jesus is ruler over all time
and space, but He limited
Himself to enter human
history at one moment of
time and one certain
place—both foretold by
prophecy.

The time God chose for my
being on earth is significant.
From Him comes my aware-
ness of the anguish caused in
our century. From Him comes
my responsibility as a world
citizen and prayer warrior in
these closing years of the sec-
ond millennium, Anno Domine.

Father God, Ruler of time and
space, show me Your purpose
for our era. Jesus, be in my
time . . .

"Come, let us return to the Lord.
He . . . will heal us . . . he will restore
us, that we may live in his presence."
                                    Hosea 6:1–2

Moses: No Ordinary Child
Acts 7:20

Jesus, be in my sonship . . .

Moses at birth was no ordinary child; even then God destined him to be the liberator. God's plan for my life includes equipping for my own unique mission as part of God's forever family.

Each stage of sonship brings unique responsibilities. The tasks I had as a child are different from the ones I have now as an adult with children of my own.

Father God, this Lent I want to act my age in Jesus, not expecting those younger in You to act beyond their own spiritual maturity quotient. Jesus, be in my sonship . . .

How great is the love the Father has lavished on us, that we should be called children of God! And that is what we are!
                    1 John 3:1

Jesus: Immanuel
Prophecy: Isaiah 7:14
Fulfillment: Matthew 1:18; Luke 1:26–35

Jesus, be in my people . . .

Immanuel, God with us, Jesus was called. God lived
among His people, experiencing their pain and sorrow,
hopes and longings, joy and laughter. It was a people
God came to seek and sanctify. I can only change myself as I seek for God to change my people.

O God, You never give up on me; may I be faithful in
caring for the people You have given me by birth and
adoption. Jesus, be in my people . . .

But you are a chosen people, a royal priesthood, a holy nation, a
people belonging to God, that you may declare the praises of him
who called you out of darkness into his wonderful light.

                                                    1 Peter 2:9

Moses: Adopted
Exodus 2:4–10

Jesus, be in my relatives . . .

When Pharaoh's daughter responded to the cry of a slave baby, her heart was responding to God's will. When Jesus' mother and brothers sought to draw Him from the crowd on the basis of their relationship, He defined what constitutes the eternal family—those who do God's will.

Father God, be in my natural relatives as I name them before You. May I respond to them in ways that give You joy. Help us also to become forever family by obedience to Your will. Jesus, be in my relatives.

"Who is my mother, and who are my brothers? . . . Whoever does the will of my Father in heaven is my brother and sister and mother."

Matthew 12:48–50

Jesus: Protected in Birth
Prophecy: Jeremiah 31:15
Fulfillment: Matthew 2:16–18

Jesus, be in my security . . .

When King Herod tried to kill the
helpless baby Jesus, an angel's warning to Joseph protected Him. Many
other times Jesus was protected from
those who tempted and threatened
Him.

Wherein is my security? In the center
of God's will. It is better to live a
brief and dangerous life in obedience to
God's call than a long, painless life
that has no significance.

Father God in whom I trust, cut me
loose from false securities that hold
me back from Your perfect plan.
Jesus, be in my security . . .

We have this hope as an anchor
for the soul, firm and secure.
                              Hebrews 6:19

Moses: Protected in Birth
Exodus 2:3, 10

Jesus, be in my salvation . . .

Moses was saved by the faith of his parents. By faith he chose to be mistreated
with the people of God. By faith he left
Egypt, not fearing the king's anger. By
faith, I join with Moses and all that "cloud
of witnesses" whose names are written in
the eleventh chapter of Hebrews.

By faith I join with Paul who ached
for the salvation of his Israeli brothers
and sisters. Father God, today my heart
aches for_____
to know Your salvation. Holy Spirit,
wash through the past, cut through
all that holds us back. Jesus, be in
my salvation.

Work out your salvation with fear and
trembling, for it is God who works in
you to will and to act according to his
good purpose.
    Philippians 2:12–13

Jesus: Refugee
Prophecy: Hosea 11:1
Fulfillment: Matthew 2:14–15

Jesus, be in my walking . . .

When Jesus' life was threatened by the evil King Herod, He and His parents became refugees in Egypt. Today Jesus still walks uncertain paths with the homeless and dispossessed. The first refugee family I met was from El Salvador, the "Savior's land": a young pastor, his plump wife and two shy children, bright black eyes peeping from behind their mother's skirts. I tried to imagine what would make them leave home, family, beloved hills and valleys, climate and culture.

God, Father of the homeless, show me how to walk with You into their need. Jesus, be in my walking . . .

To this you were called, because Christ suffered for you, leaving you an example, that you should follow in his steps.
1 Peter 2:21

Moses: Refugee
Exodus 2:15

Jesus, be in my welcoming . . .

Moses, an escaped murderer, was more
accustomed to the urban ways of Egyptian
royalty than to the simplicity of nomadic
shepherds. It was in the warmth and sincerity of the herders' welcome, however,
that he discovered home, family, and met
his God. Today, Jesus is still a stranger
among us. The answer to the desperate
needs around me does not lie in retreat,
but in thanking God and then caring for
those He sends me.

Father God, You are not threatened by impossible
situations. Show me how You expect me to be
involved. Jesus, be in my welcoming . . .

For I was hungry and you gave me something to eat, I was
thirsty and you gave me something to drink, I was a
stranger and you invited me in.   Matthew 25:35

Jesus: Light
Prophecy: Isaiah 9:1–2
Fulfillment: Matthew 4:12–16

Jesus, be in my witness . . .

Jesus began His ministry by reaching out to His neighbors.

Now as I see the hurting of my own neighbors, I want them to know Him, the Source of my joy. Still there is resistance to be overcome. I have anger at irritating ways, petty jealousies, loud music. It is so much easier to keep my distance.

Thank You, Father God, for Your faithful witnesses like Doña Julia, who urges me to invite others to prayer group. "You take your side of the street, I'll take mine," she said. Jesus, be in my witness . . .

And this is the testimony: God has given us eternal life, and this life is in his Son.   1 John 5:11

Moses: Burning Bush
Exodus 3:1–10

Jesus, be in my visions . . .

The burning bush attracted
Moses, and there he received
commissioning into God's
service. The task was only
possible with the supernatural
ingredient. In this Lenten
season I desire to meet God
daily, moment by moment
confronted with Someone
greater than my imagination,
larger than my hopes and
dreams, more powerful than
my efforts.

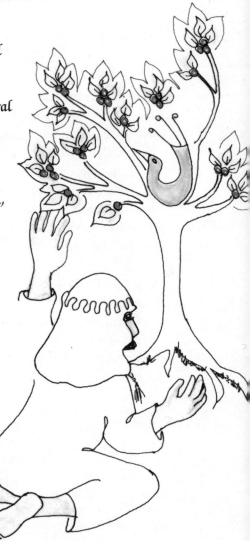

Burning Love, Consuming
Compassion give me insight
for new words and actions
that set God's people free.
Jesus, be in my visions . . .

"In the last days, God says, I
will pour out my Spirit on all
people. Your sons and daughters will prophesy, your
young men will see
visions, your old
men will dream
dreams."
        Acts 2:17–18

Jesus: Prophet
Prophecy: Deuteronomy 18:15
Fulfillment: Acts 3:19–26; John 1:45

Jesus, be in my speaking . . .

Jesus spoke with authority. His
teaching was not based on popular
opinion or scholarly learning. Every
word Jesus spoke was funneled
through God's timeless and perfect
perspective. Jesus' words exposed religious pride, reproved greed, encour-
aged the hopeless. Jesus' words,
Spirit-driven, still cut away extrane-
ous traditions.

Father God, whose Spirit is poured
out now on the earth, I want to
speak prophetic insight in practical,
down-to-earth words that strengthen,
encourage and comfort. Jesus, be in
my speaking . . .

Everyone who prophesies speaks
to men for their strengthening, encourage-
ment and comfort.   1 Corinthians 14:3

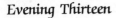

Moses: Reluctant Prophet
Exodus 4:1, 10–17

Jesus, be in my words . . .

Moses did not want to speak in front
of his people, or to Pharaoh who
hated him. God chose him anyway. I
need prophetic words in my personal
life. The body of Jesus, the Church,
also needs the clear sense of hearing
God for direction and vision. The
supernatural, holy God breaks
through my reluctance, my desire to
be in control, pointing out God's
way, giving God's words to speak.

Holy Father, God, even when I do
not desire consciously to be a channel
for Your words, speak through me,
for Your words are life and health.
Jesus, be in my words . . .

If anyone speaks, he should do it as one
speaking the very words of God . . . so that
in all things God may be praised through
Jesus Christ.   1 Peter 4:11

Jesus: Priest
Prophecy: Psalm 110:4
Fulfillment: Hebrews 5:7–10

Jesus, be in my serving . . .

Jesus demonstrated that the priest comes as a servant, the greatest willingly takes the lowest place. As high priest forever, Jesus is still among us in the outcasts of society. His presence in the filth and smells of the poor, the loneliness of the rejected and imprisoned, the agony of the sick and dying is disturbing. Why does He take the lowest place? He encourages me to respond to these needs, if not from compassion, at least from desire to minister to Him.

Father God, help me choose to help someone who is unable to help him/herself—or me! Jesus, be in my serving . . .

"Now that I, your Lord and teacher, have washed your feet, you also should wash one another's feet."
John 13:14

Moses: Priest
Exodus 4:14–17

Jesus, be in my service . . .

Although Moses felt inadequate, he was
willing to serve as mediator between God
and the people. If God calls me to do or be
something, my feelings of worth are irrele-
vant. What is important is obedience, using to the fullest what God gives me,
asking Him for more fullness, more gifts
to do the job God's way. Every believer is
a priest to the rest of Jesus' body and to
the world. Every believer can give his/her
own body as a living sacrifice.

Lord God, show me how to serve as Your presence with my family, neighbors, community, enemies in a way that delights You. Jesus, be in my
service . . .

. . . *Offer your bodies as living sacrifices, holy and pleasing
to God—which is your spiritual worship . . . be transformed
by the renewing of your mind.*
     Romans 12:1–2

Jesus: Man of Sorrows
Prophecy: Isaiah 53:3
Fulfillment: John 1:11; Luke 17:25

Jesus, be in my sorrow . . .

Even before the cross Jesus suffered the grief of being misunderstood, rejected, betrayed. His closest friends denied Him and fled in His hour of greatest need.

The disciples in the garden were so sorrowful that they were incapacitated with sleep. Sometimes the increasing troubles of the world so overwhelm me that I am overcome with helplessness and heaviness of spirit. Paul urges me to participate in Jesus' continuing sorrow, which leads to a cleansing repentance, an energizing change.

Father, wake me from the inertia of grief and bring me into creative participation in the anguish of the world. Jesus, be in my sorrow . . .

Godly sorrow brings repentance that leads to salvation and leaves no regret, but worldly sorrow brings death.
2 Corinthians 7:10

Moses: Comforts the People
Exodus 4:31

Jesus, be in my yielding . . .

After three days of sinus
headache, fighting bad
dreams and thoughts, I feel
drained. The fears and wor-
ries of poverty-stricken Nicaraguan friends pierce me
in my weakness.

How grateful I am for the comforting touch of my husband, massaging my back and praying with me, and for
this daily time of seeking God's Word. Sometimes welcoming the refugee, the poor, feels like a cross.

Father God, who cares about the suffering of Your people, use my physical and spiritual discomfort as a
training ground in trust and acceptance. Jesus, be in
my yielding . . .

Strengthen your feeble arms and weak knees. "Make level paths for
your feet," so that the lame may not be disabled, but rather healed.
Hebrews 12:12–13

Jesus: Spirit of Wisdom
Prophecy: Isaiah 11:2–4
Fulfillment: Luke 2:52; 4:18

Jesus, be in my wisdom . . .

Jesus had the Spirit of wisdom upon Him even as a twelve-year-old. Jesus knew how and when He would die, but did not resist His part in God's design.

When wisdom is at work in my life, every prayer for myself and others will be consistent with God's loving plan. I will be singleminded and stable in each task I agree to do, each group to which I choose to belong, each motive and desire. Even when stress and difficulties come, I will continue moving steadily toward the goal. This is the ideal. If I see myself wavering today, I can ask God for wisdom!

Father God, who gives generously to all, I need wisdom today. Jesus, be in my wisdom . . .

Let the word of Christ dwell in you richly as you teach and admonish one another with all wisdom. . . .
Colossians 3:16

Moses: Given Authority
Exodus 3:13–14

Jesus, be in my equipping . . .

Moses was equipped with God's Word.
God's name was his authority. When
Moses spoke that name, the people knew
they could trust and follow his leadership.
Calling on that same name, I, too, can
become equipped to fulfill the unique call
God has given me. With the help of brothers and sisters in the Lord, I discover my
gifts, the tools of my service.

Father God, shape and mold me into an
effective instrument of Your Word, Your
name, which sets enslaved people free.
Jesus, be in my equipping . . .

All Scripture is God-breathed and is useful for
teaching, rebuking, correcting and training in righteousness, so that the man of God may be thor-
oughly equipped for every good work.
                                2 Timothy 3:16–17

Jesus: King
Prophecy: Zechariah 9:9
Fulfillment: John 12:13–15;
Luke 19:28–48; Matthew 21:1–11

Jesus, be in my leaders . . .

In fulfillment of prophecy and symbol of a new kind of
Kingship, Jesus entered Jerusalem not on a war horse
but on a donkey. With the authority Jesus received
from intimate relationship with His Father, He healed
the sick and raised the dead. His was a new kind of
authority—without arrogance, without hate, without
pride or greed; instead, serving and sharing.

Father God, it is awesome to have responsibility for
others in whatever capacity, from head of household to
head of state. Lord Jesus, be in those leaders for whom
I pray today. Enable them to see those under them
with Your eyes. Jesus, be in my leaders . . .

I urge, then, first of all, that requests,
prayers, intercession and thanksgiving
be made for everyone—for kings and
all those in authority, that we may
live peaceful and quiet lives in all god-
liness and holiness.

1 Timothy 2:1–2

Moses: Accepted
Exodus 4:29–31

Jesus, be in my acceptance . . .

Moses was accepted at first by the people of Israel, but
was rejected when hardships increased. Jesus was wel-
comed as King when He rode into Jerusalem; within
days those same enthusiasts were a mob shouting,
"Crucify Him!" I cannot base my self-perception on
what others think of me. Like Moses, like Jesus, it is
better to base my being solely in an indissolvable relationship with the one true living God. I can learn from
criticism of others, without being dependent on the
positive or destroyed by the negative.

Father, reconciling God, help me to
accept Your forgiveness and love,
which penetrates even a multitude
of sins. Jesus, be in my accepting
and my acceptance . . .

Bless! Crucify!
Hosanna! Kill!
Crucify!

"I tell you the truth," he continued, "no
prophet is accepted in his home town."
                                    Luke 4:24

Jesus: Betrayed by a Friend
Prophecy: Psalm 41:9
Fulfillment: Mark 14:10–11, 43–46;
    Matthew 26:14–25

Jesus, be in my friendship . . .

Judas was trusted enough to be treasurer of the group of disciples. He had been on missions to heal the sick and preach God's Kingdom. Jesus washed Judas' feet, then shared His last meal with him. None of the disciples suspected him of being the betrayer; instead each asked anxiously, "Lord, is it I?"

Father God, how little I know my own heart. I need to lean on Jesus' breast to ask Him to show me the truth. Lord Jesus, cleanse me, wash my feet, feed me with Your body, Your blood, examine my inmost being and remove all seeds of disloyalty from me. Jesus, be in my friendship . . .

"Greater love has no one than this, that one lay down his life for his friends."   John 15:13

Moses: Opposition
Exodus 5

Jesus, be in my opposition . . .

Moses met opposition from both government leaders and his own people when he tried to carry out God's plan. God can use those who oppose me to draw me closer to Him. As I learn to pray and praise God for those who oppose me, I will grow in wisdom, grace and generosity.

The opponents of Jesus killed Him and many thousands of His followers through the centuries, but God's plan has not been thwarted. Jesus still lives and opposition proves to be fruitful ground for new life!

Father God, I release to You those who oppose what I feel is Your will. Jesus, be in my opposition . . .

In your teaching show integrity, seriousness and soundness of speech that cannot be condemned, so that those who oppose you may be ashamed because they have nothing bad to say about us.   Titus 2:7–8

Jesus: Sold for Money
Prophecy: Zechariah 11:12–13
Fulfillment: Matthew 26:14–16; 27:3–10

Jesus, be in my poverty . . .

Judas sold Jesus for money, which afterward he threw
away in horror. Paul wrote that the love of money is
the root of evil. Preoccupation with money fills up
those interior spaces that belong to God, the inner core
that needs to be full of praise and adoration of God,
trusting in His provision. Just before Judas betrayed
Jesus, he saw the widow give all she had. Even though
the leaders of the Temple were corrupt and doubtless
held in contempt the widow's meager contribution,
Jesus praised her generosity.

All-seeing Lord God, cleanse me of false motives. Free
me to dedicate all my money and resources to Your
service. Jesus, be in my poverty . . .

"She out of her poverty put in all she had to live on."

Luke 21:4

Moses: Work Increased
Exodus 5:7ff.

Jesus, be in my burdens . . .

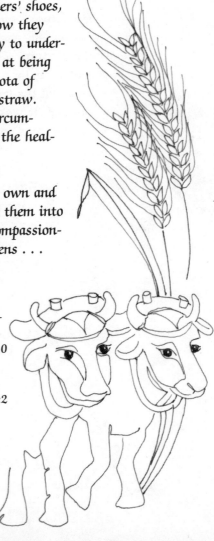

When I try to put myself in others' shoes,
many times I cannot imagine how they
bear so much pressure. It is easy to understand the Israelites' desperation at being
ordered to turn out the same quota of
bricks while also gathering the straw.
They could not see that their circum-
stances had to get worse before the healing could come.

Father God, as I pray about my own and
others' burdens, help me release them into
Your all-knowing, all-loving, compassionate hands. Jesus, be in my burdens . . .

"Come to me, all you who are weary
and burdened, and I will give you
rest. . . . My yoke is easy and my bur-
den is light."

Matthew 11:28–30

Carry each other's burdens.

Galatians 6:2

Jesus: Betrayed by Religious Leaders
Prophecy: Zechariah 11:13
Fulfillment: Matthew 27:3–10

Jesus, be in my persecutors . . .

The false shepherds demanded the death of the
Good Shepherd. They were afraid that Jesus
would overturn not just a few tables in the Temple court, but their entire system, their concept of
God and the power structure from which they
profited. It was easier to get rid of the sinless
One than to expose their own sin and ignorance
of the God whose name they used.

Father God, invisible, almighty, keep
me from blindness and hardness of
heart. If I am judged and condemned
in small ways or great for having a
vibrant relationship with You, I give
You praise. Jesus, be in
my persecutors . . .

Bless those who persecute you; bless and do
not curse. . . . Do not be overcome by evil,
but overcome evil with good.
Romans 12:14, 21

Moses: Plagues Sent
Exodus 7:14–10:20

Jesus, be in my calamities . . .

One disaster after another
came upon the Egyptians, but
they could not hear God's voice
saying, "Let my people go."
The Bible is full of examples of
natural disasters as well as
enemy armies directed or allowed by God to call individu-
als and nations to turn to Him.
Those who seek God find an
intimate love relation in the
midst of calamities. The prophets, who were blameless of the
sins of the people, participated
with the people in their suffering even while interceding for
their relief.

Father God, help me see the
disasters in life from Your perspective, and to thank You
even before I do. Jesus, be in
my calamities . . .

I will take refuge in the shadow of
your wings until the disaster has
passed. . . .   Psalm 57:1

Abortion
Contamination
Racism
Radiation
Homeless
AIDS
Alienation
Starvation
WAR
Floods
drought
Pesticides
Oil Spills
Acid Rain
Nuclear
Holocaust

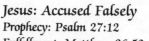

Jesus: Accused Falsely
Prophecy: Psalm 27:12
Fulfillment: Matthew 26:59–68

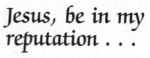

Jesus, be in my reputation . . .

Even though Jesus had done nothing wrong, there were many who came forward to accuse Him falsely. Words are swords, which the Holy Spirit uses only to heal, but which the accuser of the brethren uses to wound and destroy.

It is Jesus' way to know the worst about me and to care enough to cover me with costly love and forgiveness. That must be my way toward the ones who accuse me.

Father God, when I am accused, give me that single-eyed devotion that cares only for my standing with You. Jesus, be in my reputation . . .

He was assigned a grave with the wicked
. . . though he had done no violence. . . .
                                          Isaiah 53:9

Moses: Plague of
Darkness
Exodus 10:21–29

Jesus, be in my darkness . . .

The ninth plague on Egypt, when
Pharaoh refused to let the people go,
was that of darkness—everywhere
except in the ghetto that housed the
children of Israel. Jesus said His followers are to shine—not just as a reflec-
tion of His light, but to *be* light in the
world's darkness. In His light is high
visibility to see things as they are. In
His light is forgiveness and fellowship.
Sometimes in an attentive moment I
can see light around another person,
allowing me to see him/her as close to
God, holy.

Father of Light, illumine my thoughts,
plans, motives. Shine on those around
me today the light of Jesus, Sun of
Righteousness risen with healing rays.
Jesus, be in my darkness . . .

God is light; in him there is no
darkness at all.
        1 John 1:5

Jesus: Sacrificial Lamb
Prophecy: Isaiah 53:7; Psalm 38:13–15
Fulfillment: Matthew 26:62; 27:12–14

Jesus, be in my sacrifice . . .

Once at a camp in the North Carolina mountains, we had a Passover
celebration using a real lamb. The
living lamb playing in the lush
green pasture was soft and woolly,
a bit shy, but consenting to eat
grass out of our hands. The lamb
met death without bleat or cry,
still trusting us. Stripped of its
fleece and tied to a pole to drain
the blood, the lamb's body vividly
reminded us of Jesus torn and
bleeding on the cross.

Father God, who gave Your most
precious Son, Jesus, on the cross,
thank You for showing that the
way of fullness of joy is in giving
my own life away without grum-
bling or complaining. Jesus, be in
my sacrifice . . .

Offer your bodies as living sacrifices, holy
and pleasing to God—which is your spiritual worship.   Romans 12:1

Moses: Passover Lamb
Exodus 12:29

Jesus, be in my obedience . . .

Pharaoh was so enmeshed in grandiose plans, which
his Hebrew slaves enabled him to execute, that he
could not see God's still greater plan. Even Pharaoh's
punishment prefigured God's redemptive design: the
death of His first-born. Every warning, every punishment, every catastrophe can be used for God's purpose,
to bring me to the place of obedience. Every way leads
to death, but only one way leads through it, and Jesus
is the Way!

God, kind and merciful Father,
help me not to pursue blindly
my own plans and goals, but to
choose always the way that
leads home to You. Jesus, be in
my obedience . . .

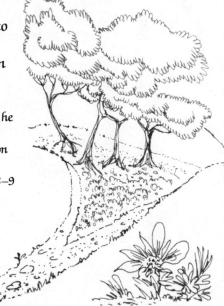

(Jesus) learned obedience from what he
suffered and, once made perfect, he
became the source of eternal salvation
for all who obey him. . . .
                          Hebrews 5:8–9

Jesus: Wounded Healer
Prophecy: Isaiah: 53:4–5
Fulfillment: Matthew 8:16–17

Jesus, be in my healing . . .

It is by Jesus' wounds that I receive healing. In turn,
Jesus transforms my wounds into compassion that
heals others. He wants me to help others give their
woundedness to Him. Maybe they do not see His
pierced hands reaching out in love to them. Maybe
they have not heard of His love in a way that embold-
ens them to unmask their pain.

Father God, Creator and Healer,
thank You for the wounds of the
past. Thank You for Your consistent,
persistent healing touch where I need
it. Use me as an instrument of Your
wholeness. Jesus, be in my healing . . .

"It is Jesus' name and the faith that comes
through him that has given this complete
healing to him."   Acts 3:16

By his wounds you have been healed.
                                    1 Peter 2:24

Moses: Passover: Blood of Life
Exodus 12:13

Jesus, be in my life . . .

The life is in the blood. The blood
of Abel cried out from the ground
for revenge. The blood of Jesus
cries out, "Father, forgive them."
It is the blood of Jesus, of the
Passover Lamb, that is placed in
the form of a cross on the door-
posts of my heart, sign of God's
total ownership and deliverance.
Death has no sting because in Jesus' death I have entered already
into death to my willful self.

Father God, thank You for Jesus'
willingness to pour out His life's
blood for me. Jesus, be in my
life . . .

We have confidence to enter the Most
Holy Place by the blood of Jesus.
                               Hebrews 10:19

Jesus: Hated
Prophecy: Psalm 69:4; 109:3–5
Fulfillment: John 15:23–25

Jesus, be in my enemies . . .

Those who care enough to be angry with me are moving on a track that can change us both. Perhaps there is legitimate cause for this enmity I provoke. If I do not stiffen in my position, become rigid and unbending, then perhaps I can find a way to change what is wrong and irritating in myself, get the log out of my own eye and open the way for reconciliation. Even if that does not work, I am better for having had to face the enemy's wrath and respond with compassion.

Father God, Author of reconciliation, I lift to You both my suffering and the enemy who caused it. Draw us into Your cleansing love. Free us of every bondage that keeps us from relationship in You. Jesus, be in my enemies . . .

"But I tell you who hear me: Love your enemies, do good to those who hate you, bless those who curse you, pray for those who mistreat you."   Luke 6:27–28

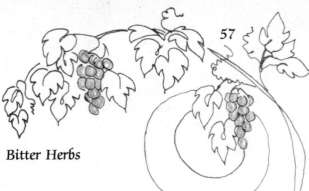

Moses: Passover: Bitter Herbs
Exodus 12:7–8

Jesus, be in my testing . . .

Jesus took a broken piece of bread and dipped it into
the bitter herb, horseradish, and the charoseth, a sweet
sauce of chopped apples, nuts, cinnamon and wine.
Charoseth represents the red clay mortar used in making bricks in Egypt, the herb their bitter forced labor—
sweetened by the coming redeemer. At this point in the
Passover meal Jesus said to Judas, "Do what you must
do quickly." The hour of testing had come for all of
them.

Father God, You test me to show my need for total
dependence on You. Through the bitterness of life's
experience, show me Your sweet redemption. Jesus, be
the in my testing . . .

Consider it pure joy . . . whenever you face
trials of many kinds, because you know that
the testing of your faith develops persever-
ance.   James 1:2–3

Jesus: Unresisting
Prophecy: Isaiah 53:6, 12
Fulfillment: 1 Corinthians 15:3

Jesus, be in my cross . . .

Without complaining or retaliating, Jesus submitted
Himself to self-righteous, corrupt religious and political leaders and to a crazed mob. Jesus took from every
human being the penalty of the sin nature. When I am
in that place God designed for me, bound to the agony
of my own cross, I am in the healing stream that
flows from the love that lays down its life for others.

Father God, I yield to You all that holds
me back from the cross You designed for
me. I receive it, Lord, as good for me. Jesus, be in my cross . . .

He himself bore our sins in his body on
the tree, so that we might die to sin and
live for righteousness.   1 Peter 2:24

Moses: Passover: Unleavened Bread
Exodus 12:14–20

Jesus, be in my hunger . . .

My hunger is both physical and spiritual, and Jesus cares about both. The pure, unleavened bread of sincerity and truth is the body of Jesus Himself, which becomes part of me as I take Him into myself in Communion. When Jesus had compassion on the hungry crowds, He fed as well as healed them, and expected His disciples to do the same.

Father God of abundant provision, feed me today daily bread and the ever renewed nourishment of Your presence. I want to be Your disciple who feeds others, meeting their hunger with Your good gifts. Jesus, be in my hunger . . .

Get rid of the old yeast that you may be a new batch without yeast—as you really are. For Christ, our Passover Lamb, has been sacrificed.   1 Corinthians 5:7

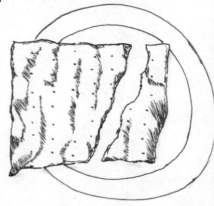

Jesus: Mocked
Prophecy: Isaiah 50:6
Fulfillment: Mark 14:65; 15:17–20; John 18:22; 19:1–3

Jesus, be in my reproach . . .

Only rarely have I experienced ridicule or contempt, nothing close to Jesus' ordeal, but I have known Christians mocked and tortured for their faith. I cannot predict if and when these trials will come or from whom or how I will react. The important thing is to handle the daily tests in Jesus' Spirit, so as to be ready for the "final exam."

Father God, my Keeper, keep me steady in times when others despise me because of You. Let Jesus' actions be my reactions. Let me see Jesus in those who reproach me for You are their Lord even if they do not yet know You. Jesus, be in my reproach . . .

If you are insulted because of the name of Christ, you are blessed, for the Spirit of glory and of God rests on you.   1 Peter 4:14

Moses: Passover: Charoseth
Exodus 5:6–21

Jesus, be in my work . . .

The charoseth on the Passover table
stands for the bricks that the children of
Israel were forced to manufacture in
Egypt. God's people were enslaved to a
taskmaster who expected more than they
could give. In God's plan, work is a
holy joy. God does not expect more
than I can do. Sometimes I can do
more than I think possible, but
only when I work in freedom, not
in slavery.

Infinitely caring Father God,
stand with those trapped today
under unholy burdens, work
that destroys rather than re-
creates, under taskmasters
whose god is other than the
Lover of their souls. Jesus,
be in my work . . .

. . . Each will be rewarded according to his own labor. For
we are God's fellow workers. . . .
                    1 Corinthians 3:8–9

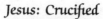

Jesus: Crucified
Prophecy: Psalm 22:14–17; Isaiah 53:12
Fulfillment: Galatians 5:24–25; 6:2

Jesus, be in my crucifixion . . .

In God's economy, when I choose to be dead to an area that is unhealthy for me, He opens up fullness of life, pours out His Spirit's power, which enables me to do and be far more than I could imagine. That is *grace!* Grace enables me to see others fall under their burdens and know that it could be I. Grace enables me to help others with their burdens and allow others to help me.

Father God, full of grace and truth, put to death in me all that rises against You. Bring to life all those possibilities that You see in me. Jesus, be in my crucifixion . . .

Those who belong to Christ Jesus have crucified the sinful nature with its passions and desires. . . . Carry each other's burdens, and in this way you will fulfill the law of Christ.   Galatians 5:24; 6:2

Moses: Passover: Meaning
Psalm 113

Jesus, be in my religion . . .

True Hebrews viewed faith as relationship and response to God, not as correct actions or intellectual
acceptance of certain facts. Jesus reminded His disciples of their heritage during the Passover meal, His
last supper. His was an ancient religion made new
constantly by the breath of God's Holy Spirit. He calls
me to a "religion" careful with words, generous with
orphans and widows and cautious about the deceptive
culture of the world.

Father God, Spirit and Truth, I need Your gift of dis-
cernment to distinguish those parts of my life that are
merely "religious observance" from those that respond
to Your lively presence. Jesus, be in my religion . . .

Religion that God our Father accepts as pure and faultless is this:
to look after orphans and widows in their distress and, to keep
oneself from being polluted by the world.   James 1:27

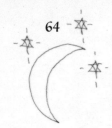

Jesus: Pierced
Prophecy: Psalm 22:16; Zechariah 12:10
Fulfillment: John 19:36–37; 20:25–27

Jesus, be in my anguish . . .

Zechariah saw by the Spirit whole Jewish families, entire tribes of Israel, the city of Jerusalem itself filled with mourning for this One who was pierced. The anguish would open up a fountain that would cleanse away all sin, impurity and false worship. In the meantime, all creation is in travail, as a woman in labor, yearning, working for the birthing of the sons of God.

Father God, who allowed the suffering of Your beloved Son, today I pray urgently for the Pierced One to be revealed not only to my own loved ones, but to all Jewish people. Jesus, be in my anguish . . .

"A woman giving birth to a child has pain because her time has come; but when her baby is born she forgets the anguish because of her joy that a child is born into the world."   John 16:21

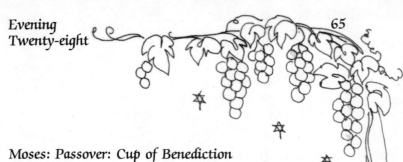

Moses: Passover: Cup of Benediction
Psalm 115

Jesus, be in my blessing . . .

At the Passover table Jesus blessed the third cup, the
cup of benediction, and prayed for His disciples and for
all who would come to believe in Him. His blessing
rests on me today and on all who are grafted into Jesus
the vine. As I stretch out my arms to embrace the Pas-
siontide, as I reach from the passion of Jesus on the
cross to Easter, I am blessed and enabled to be a
blessing.

"Blessed art Thou, O Lord our God, who hast created
the fruit of the vine. . . . Blessed art Thou, O Lord our
God, who has sustained us and enabled us to reach
this season." Enable me to be a blessing till He comes
again. Jesus, be in my blessing . . .

"I am the vine; you are the branches.
If a man remains in me and
I in him, he will bear much fruit."
                    John 15:5

Jesus: Insulted
Prophecy: Psalm 22:6–8
Fulfillment: Matthew 27:39–44; Mark 15:29–32

Jesus, be in my rebuke . . .

There was no basis for the insults hurled at Jesus.
There was no truth to the rebukes and no way He
could be any different and still be true to His heavenly Father. Often, however, there is much I can
learn when criticism is flung at me—even in anger.
Rather than react in defensiveness and with like
words, I can choose to listen and learn from the
kernel of truth in the rebuke.

Thank You, Father God, for Your
Word, which instructs and rebukes
me, equipping me for every good
work. Help me receive the truth
and reject the false from those who
criticize me. Jesus, be in my rebuke . . .

"Whoever corrects a mocker invites in-
sult. . . . Rebuke a wise man and he will
love you."   Proverbs 9:7–8

Moses: Passover: Praise
Psalm 135

Jesus, be in my praise . . .

Jesus taught that the twin tools for overcoming evil
are prayer and praise, linked with steady commitment
to the poor. Moses knew that, too, as he showed the
Israelites in the Goshen slums how to celebrate the
first Passover in prayer and thanksgiving. Later,
Miriam, Moses' sister, acted out
Moses' song of praise by taking
a tambourine and leading the
women in a dance of joy.

Father God, worthy to be
praised, today I thank You for
these moments of quiet in the
secret place alone with You. It
is not easy to face those who
despise me for loving You.
Jesus, be in my praise . . .

Through Jesus, therefore, let us continually offer to God a sacrifice of
praise—the fruit of lips that confess
his name.   Hebrews 13:15

Jesus: Thirsty
Prophecy: Psalm 69:21
Fulfillment: John 19:28–29; Matthew 27:34, 48

Jesus, be in my thirst . . .

The woman was drawing water from the well when
she met Jesus. He had living water for the asking, yet
was thirsty Himself. This is a paradox. Even when I
am in touch with the Source of all creation and cre-
ativity, flowing in that stream of healing power, a
channel for marvelous gifts of God to others, I may be
weak and in need of help.

Father God, who satisfies
my thirsting spirit, lead me
to the Living Water. Show
me which books to read,
which teachers to heed,
which groups to join as I
live, move, have my being
in You. Jesus, be in my
thirst . . .

"Blessed are those who hunger
and thirst for righteousness, for
they will be filled."

Matthew 5:6

Moses: Passover: the Final Cup
Psalm 118

Jesus, be in my remembrance . . .

Jesus did not drink the fourth and final cup of the
Passover with His disciples at the Last Supper. There
will be a wedding feast and the fourth cup of wine
that is already poured will be drunk with Him in the
company of all who put their con-
fidence in Him. While I await this
glorious meal, the Holy Spirit
brings to my remembrance what
Jesus taught.

Father God, Lord of the new
heavens and earth as well as
our broken and wounded world
today, bring to my mind all that
I need to know of Jesus' words.
Bring into my experience what I
need to draw others to desire to
share this blessed feast with
You. Jesus, be in my remembrance . . .

I thank my God every time I remember
you.   Philippians 1:3

Jesus: Rejected
Prophecy: Psalm 22:6–8
Fulfillment: Matthew 27:43

Jesus, be in my rejection . . .

Rejection is a destructive force, an open door to the destroyer. When I am rejected, wounds are made that only love can heal. A person rejected repeatedly early in life ceases to believe that he/she is acceptable. The rejected person invites more rejection in a vicious downward spiral. God's unconditional love in Jesus can break through and open the door to healthy relationships of giving and receiving. Jesus took on Himself all rejection so that I can be freed of its consequences, free to love myself and even those who reject themselves.

Father God, as I am warmed in Your acceptance today, give me Your love for _____.
I come against the spirit of rejection in the powerful name of Jesus.
Jesus, be in my rejection . . .

For everything God created is good, and nothing is to be rejected if it is received with thanksgiving.
1 Timothy 4:4

Moses:
Departure from Egypt
Exodus 12:31–42

Jesus, be in my journey . . .

After 430 years in Egypt, it was
God's time to move out. It is not
always easy to discern His path.
Jim says that God often allows us
more than one path, requiring us
to choose. After I have sought God
individually and provided Jim with all
the insight available to me, then we
have followed the path Jim chose.
Though at the time we often felt
abandoned and blind, looking back
we can clearly see God's direction.

Thank You, Father God, Light in
the darkness, for Your faithful
leading. Jesus, be in my
journey . . .

Your word is a lamp to my feet and a
light for my path.
              Psalm 119:105

Jesus: Prayed for Our Forgiveness
Prophecy: Psalm 109:1–4
Fulfillment: Luke 23:34

Jesus, be in my prayer . . .

David was a man of prayer, but his prayer was that those who had done evil to him be destroyed. How unlike Jesus that is! Certainly I understand David's feelings of anger at deception and betrayal. David saw himself as innocent, wounded and completely justified in seeking his enemies' destruction. History indicates, however, that the very evil he wished on his opponent came back on him. Jesus' prayer was, "Father, forgive them."

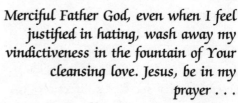

Merciful Father God, even when I feel justified in hating, wash away my vindictiveness in the fountain of Your cleansing love. Jesus, be in my prayer . . .

"But if you do not forgive men their sins, your Father will not forgive your sins."
Matthew 6:15

Moses: Pillar of Cloud
Exodus 13:21

Jesus, be in my protection . . .

What I might imagine as "safe" could
be dangerous for me; the only perfect
protection is in the center of God's will.
In the journey to the Promised Land,
though there were discomforts and
struggles on the way, God's will for
His children included victory over
enemies, provision of daily bread,
health—even shoes that didn't
wear out!

Father God, watchful Guardian
through the night, show me where I
have strayed from Your design. Put
my feet squarely on the path You
choose for me. Jesus, be in my
protection . . .

"My prayer is not that you take
them out of the world but that you
protect them from the evil one."
                    John 17:15

Jesus: Intercessor
Prophecy: Isaiah 53:12
Fulfillment: Luke 23:34

Jesus, be in my intercession . . .

Intercession goes beyond asking, "What
can I do to help?" It means I become
willing to be a part of the answer. Intercession can be like the agony of
childbirth, which has a rhythm of push-
ing followed by passive waiting. Intercession is participation with God in the
creative process of birthing and bringing
sons and daughters of God to maturity.

Father God, who yearns for
each of Your creatures with
terrible, tender love, give me
an intercessor's heart. Jesus,
be in my intercession . . .

He is able to save completely those
who come to God through him,
because he always lives to intercede
for them.   Hebrews 7:25

Moses: Pursuit
Exodus 14:1–9

Jesus, be in my fleeing . . .

The children of Israel fled from cruel slavery and from the demands of pagan Pharaoh. Paul teaches that I, too, am to flee from every bondage that chains me to any will other than God's. He has erected His road signs of justice, faith, love and peace to point the way to freedom. The enslaved Israelis, whose only hope was God, united to refuse the will of the powerful. All the weapons of war aimed against them were destroyed by the same waters that God opened wide to save His people.

Father God, set free those
bound in poverty, addictions,
passions as I name them.
Jesus, be in my fleeing . . .

Flee the evil desires of youth, and
pursue righteousness, faith, love and
peace.   2 Timothy 2:22

Jesus: Firstborn Son Pierced
Prophecy: Zechariah 12:10
Fulfillment: John 19:34

Jesus, be in my dying . . .

The dying, inert, helpless figure of Jesus on the cross represents my death to things of my own choosing—dreams, ambitions, projected enjoyments and the sin that inevitably comes with my own way. Jesus took it all.

Jesus' victory was over all the forces of death. I am with Him in new, full, vibrant life even when I don't feel like it. "Don't despair," Paul encourages. Don't give up the fight, because in Jesus' victory you have won and will win. In Jesus is no condemnation.

Abba, Daddy, I give to You everything that is death to me, and welcome dying in order to live. Jesus, be in my dying . . .

Count yourselves dead to sin but alive to God in Christ Jesus.   Romans 6:11

Moses: Deliverance
Exodus 14:13–14

Jesus, be in my deliverance . . .

God made a way where there was no way. Every
suffering people from then on could claim the way
God led His people out of Egypt as their own
promise of deliverance. In God's timing and
miraculous manner are liberation,
release, fulfillment, both individually and as groups of believers.

I am to be an instrument of deliverance as well, strengthening the
weak, welcoming the lonely and
displaced. If I have not experienced
deliverance myself, I cannot be a
channel for it to flow to others.

Father God, Liberator and righteous
Judge, in You alone is escape from
pressures. In You alone is victory
over powers not of You. Jesus, be in
my deliverance . . .

The Lord will rescue me from every
evil attack and will bring me safely
to his heavenly kingdom.
            2 Timothy 4:18

Jesus: Naked
Prophecy: Psalm 22:17–18
Fulfillment: Mark 15:24; John 19:24

Jesus, be in my shame . . .

Jesus was exposed on the cross—in a culture
where nakedness was shameful. He was
willing to experience shame to free from
shame all who look to Him.

When I fear exposure, fear what
others think, when I have something to hide, I am failing to avail
myself of this freedom. When I give
to God all I am, weaknesses as well
as strengths, they are no longer
mine. Then my shame can be used
for His glory.

Father God, Lifter of my head, I
want to be totally open before You,
no hidden places except in You, my
Hiding Place. Jesus, be in my
shame . . .

The apostles left the
Sanhedrin, rejoicing be-
cause they had been counted
worthy of suffering disgrace
for the Name.
Acts 5:41

Moses: Bitter Water
Exodus 15:23–27

Jesus, be in my pressing on . . .

God's people had just exulted over their great victory over Pharaoh when they were confronted with a spring of bitter water in the desert. So they grumbled to Moses, who cried out to God. The water was made sweet in answer to his prayer.

Father God, Lord of the journey, when I am confronted by bitterness after experiencing Your victory, help me cry out to You with the confident faith of Moses. Jesus, be in my pressing on . . .

I press on toward the goal to win the prize for which God has called me heavenward in Christ Jesus.   Philippians 3:14

Jesus: Protected in Death
Prophecy: Psalm 34:19–20; Exodus 12:43, 46–47
Fulfillment: John 19:31–33

Jesus, be in my bones . . .

That Jesus' bones would not be broken in His
death was prophesied long before David.

Every part of me is important to God. My
bones were knit together in my mother's
womb under God's loving supervision.
Bones are nourished by awe of
the Lord, and conscious turn-
ing away from evil (Proverbs
3:7–8). Discerning, understanding,
wise words bring strength to the
bones.

Father God, my bones, my
being, I place in Your hands
for healing. Jesus, be in my
bones . . .

Pleasant words are a honey-
comb, sweet to the soul and
healing to the bones.
Proverbs 16:24

Moses: Manna
Exodus 16:14–15

Jesus, be in my provision . . .

God wants His people to have what is
needed to sustain life. In the desert
God's people were dependent on Him for
daily provision. In the Promised Land
where they grew fat in abundance, they
forgot the Source of supply and followed
other gods.

Father God, Source of all good, in my poverty I seek
You as my only provision. In my abundance I seek You
as my only treasure. Keep me from ingratitude and
forgetfulness. Jesus, be in my provision . . .

Our people must learn to devote themselves to doing what is
good, in order that they may provide for daily necessities and not
live unproductive lives.   Titus 3:14

Jesus: Buried
Prophecy: Isaiah 53:9
Fulfillment: Matthew 27:57–60

Jesus, be in my burial . . .

From this side of the grave there is an awesome finality to death. The strong witness of Scripture is that
in baptism I am buried to the earth-life with Christ.
Everything in me in opposition to God is interred, null
and void, powerless. Only then can resurrection life
take over. Paul said he died daily in order to live continually that resurrection-empowered life.

Father God, Lord of the living and
the dead, show me those things in
me that need to be buried with
finality today. Jesus, be in my
burial . . .

We were therefore buried with him
through baptism into death in order
that . . . we too may live a new life.
Romans 6:4

Moses: Water from Rock
Exodus 17:1–7

Jesus, be in my crying . . .

The children of Israel wandering in the wilderness day after day had no personal contact with God. Their go-between was Moses. When there was no water they cried to Moses instead of to their heavenly Father who loved them.

In Jesus we have boldness to approach God directly. In the midst of necessity, confronted by the impossible, I can cry out to God, Abba, Daddy, trusting that God's love will provide what is needed.

Father God, who hears the cries of my heart, when others look to me as their source, help me, with shining face, point them to You as their Provider and Guide. Jesus, be in my crying . . .

Because you are sons, God sent the Spirit of his Son into our hearts, the Spirit who calls out, "Abba, Father."   Galatians 4:6

Jesus: Resurrection
Prophecy: Psalm 16:9–10; Matthew 16:21
Fulfillment: Matthew 28:5–10; Luke 24:36–48

Jesus, be in my future . . .

For the believer, the future is in God's loving hands, therefore not to be feared. Jesus lived in confidence that God is in control, even though He knew that ahead were rejection and death. Paul knew he would be murdered by an unjust political system, but certainty of the resurrection enabled him to minister confidently.

Father God, who claims me, the future is a vast unknown to me. You know the future, though, and You know me and You have chosen the best for me. Jesus, be in my future . . .

For I am convinced that neither death nor life, neither angels nor demons, neither the present nor the future . . . will be able to separate us from the love of God that is in Christ Jesus our Lord.
Romans 8:38

Moses: No Other Gods
Exodus 20:1–3

Jesus, be in my worship . . .

God gave His children ten
essential rules through Moses.
Jesus distilled them into
two: love God with all my
heart, soul, mind, and my
neighbor as myself.

To love God, who is love,
begins with denying any
other gods. To love God
alone is to worship in
God's Spirit, led by the
Spirit, ministering the
Spirit's gifts.

Father God, Maker of
the universe, You alone
deserve my allegiance.
Wash me free of any
conscious or unconscious
idolatry that takes away
from our love. Jesus, be
in my worship . . .

"God is spirit, and his wor-
shipers must worship in spirit
and in truth."   John 4:24

Jesus: Ascension
Prophecy: Psalm 68:18
Fulfillment: Luke 24:50–53; Acts 1:9–11

Jesus, be in my revelations . . .

After forty days of marvelous communion with the resurrected Jesus,
the disciples watched Him ascend
into the heavens. Ten days later,
the Holy Spirit of Jesus descended
upon them. The history of the
Church is the record of the same
fire of the Holy Spirit breaking out
in every generation in revelations,
wisdom, prophecy, healings,
miracles. He is alive!

Father God, reveal my part in Your
great plan. Prepare me, fill me, use
me. Reveal what pleases You.
Jesus, be in my revelations . . .

I keep asking that the God of our
Lord Jesus Christ, the glorious Father, may give you the Spirit of
wisdom and revelation, so that you
may know him better.
Ephesians 1:17

Moses: Sabbath Holy
Exodus 20:8

Jesus, be in my rest . . .

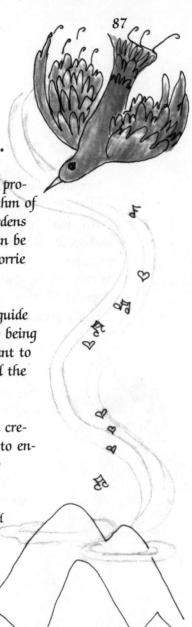

God rested on the seventh day and provided a rest for me within the rhythm of
His life. When I struggle with burdens
that are not mine to carry there can be
no rest. "Nestle, don't wrestle," Corrie
ten Boom advised.

God speaks through His Word to guide
me to the work He has for me. By being
available to the Holy Spirit resistant to
other demands, the apostles turned the
world upside down!

Father God who has done it all in creation and in salvation, enable me to enter into Your rest. Jesus, be in my
rest . . .

"Come to me, all you who are weary and
burdened, and I will give you rest."
      Matthew 11:28

Jesus' Last Words: "Father, Forgive Them"
Luke 23:34

Jesus, be in my forgiveness . . .

"They don't know what they are doing," Jesus said of
His torturers. Some of those were maliciously evil,
others merely caught up in mob spirit, still others on-
lookers too weak to protest, a few simply doing their
duty. Jesus forgave them all. He expects me to follow
His example so that He can freely forgive me. My forgiveness of others is the key that opens the door into
God's presence. This day I can sit in God's lap, be
hugged and know I am forgiven.

Father, examine my heart. Uncover any
bitterness that cannot stand the light of
Your love. Reveal it and wash me free to
be fully in You. Jesus, be in my
forgiveness . . .

Bear with each other and forgive whatever
grievances you may have against one another.
Forgive as the Lord forgave you.
Colossians 3:13

Moses: God's Name Holy
Exodus 20:7

Jesus, be in my language . . .

God's name represents His very person,
nature, power. In Jesus' name mighty miracles and healings are accomplished. There
is power in that name. What is most precious and holy has always been subject to
ridicule and misuse, both casually and
intentionally blasphemous. As I learn to
guard my words that they may be a
stream of blessing and healing to others,
my use of God's name will take on more
meaning and power.

Holy Father God, Holy Jesus,
Holy Spirit of God, teach me
to honor Your name with my
mouth and with a manner
of living that demonstrates
Your nature to unbelievers.
Jesus, be in my language . . .

"This is how you should pray: 'Our
Father in heaven, hallowed be your
name.' "   Matthew 6:9

Jesus: "Today in Paradise"
Luke 23:43

Jesus, be in my saving . . .

Even on the cross Jesus invited the two thieves to
come with Him into paradise. One accepted, the other
ridiculed the offer. Even bound in His suffering, Jesus'
caring reached out to embrace those around Him. The
response of each to Him was a matter of life and
death. Today it is the same. As Jesus' representative, I
need to go beyond anger at injustice and pity for those
suffering; I must extend Your life-giving invitation.

O Lord God, as I look at Jesus on the cross, welcoming the thief to paradise, I know You have rescued me,
too. Show me those whom You would draw into Your
Kingdom through me today. Jesus, be in my saving . . .

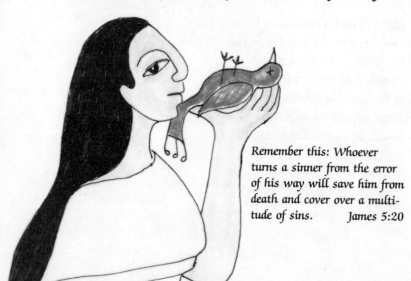

Remember this: Whoever
turns a sinner from the error
of his way will save him from
death and cover over a multitude of sins.   James 5:20

Moses: No Idols
Exodus 20:4

Jesus, be in my living . . .

Immorality, impurity and greed are idols, Paul says, just as much as a golden calf. The Ten Commandments focus on the negative, Jesus on the positive. The opposite of immorality is healthy appreciation of other persons and myself as holy creations of God. The opposite of impurity is mind, mouth, body washed with God's living words. The opposite of greed is glad sharing.

Father God, ever-living and ever-creating, create in me a clean heart, a new song, a gracious spirit. In any area where I am deceived and worshiping some god other than You, shine the light of Your truth into my darkness. Jesus, be in my living . . .

No immoral, impure or greedy person—such a man is an idolater—has any inheritance in the kingdom of Christ and of God.   Ephesians 5:5

Jesus: Honored His Mother
John 19:26–27

Jesus, be in my mother . . .

The last act of Jesus on the cross was to ask John, His
beloved disciple, to care for Mary, His mother. Jesus
had other brothers who could have been responsible,
but Jesus wanted His mother's last years to be with
the "disciple of love."

In his old age, John wrote three letters of love to all
believers. He had learned of this costly love in three
years of walking with Jesus and in caring for Mary
after Jesus' death.

Father God, who placed me in a family,
show me how You would have me care for
my mother and all You have entrusted to
my care. Jesus, be in my mother . . .

"Honor your father and
your mother."
Exodus 20:12

Moses: Honor Parents
Exodus 20:12

Jesus, be in my father . . .

The Law of Moses promised blessing on those who
honor their earthly father and mother. Jesus fulfilled
that Law, then put it into new perspective. God alone
has the rights and privileges of fatherhood. When I
recognize God as Father, my earthly relationships cease
to be bondage, and are filled with supernatural love,
greater than ever before. In God's family, forgiving love
spills over the lines of ancestry and race, and widens
our opportunities to love.

Thank You, Father God, for my earthly
father, whose love enabled me to come
into being and to grow into a woman able
to love. Thank You for spiritual fathers
who have led me to You. Warmly and
richly bless them . . .

We dealt with each of you as a father
deals with his own children.
                        1 Thessalonians 2:11

Jesus: Forsaken
Matthew 27:46

Jesus, be in my silence . . .

Jesus enjoyed perfect communion with His Father, yet on the cross He was forsaken, encountered silent skies. The impenetrable weight of the sins of the world, my sins, separated Jesus from the loving Father. Communication was cut off from Him to open intimacy for me.

On the cross, Jesus overcame the terror of silence, as He overcame every evil. Now, after the cross, heaven's seeming silence is an invitation to listen, to plunge deeper into the vast resources available in God. As with lovers who are secure in their acceptance, silence speaks of being together without barriers, without walls, without need to impress, available . . .

Father God, so many times I struggle to hear You. Calm me, for only in my own silence can I hear Your still, quiet voice. Jesus, be in my silence . . .

The Lord is in his holy temple; let all the earth be silent before him.

Habakkuk 2:20

Moses: "Do Not Murder"
Exodus 20:13

Jesus, be in my anger . . .

Jesus taught that murder has roots in anger. I cannot
be totally free of anger, but I can learn to prevent anger from killing. Psychologists say that anger held in-
side festers into depression. Anger expressed to God
loses its destructive quality. God shows me where I
can channel those energies in constructing His Kingdom, combatting the demonic powers that oppose Him.

Thank You, Father God, omnipotent Ruler of the universe, that You understand my anger, frustrations that
lash out to wound others. Forgive me, Lord. Fit me
with Jesus' armor for the cosmic battle. Jesus, be in my
anger . . .

Get rid of all bitterness, rage and anger. . . . Be kind and compassionate to
one another, forgiving."
Ephesians 4:31–32

Jesus: "I Thirst"
John 19:28

Jesus, be in my fast . . .

"Is not this the kind of fasting I
have chosen: to loose the chains
of injustice and untie the cords
of the yoke. . . ? Is it not to
share your food with the hungry
and to provide the poor wan-
derer with shelter[?] . . . If you
do away with the yoke of op-
pression, with the pointing fin-
ger and malicious talk, and if
you spend yourselves in behalf
of the hungry and satisfy the
needs of the oppressed, then
your light will rise in the darkness, and your night will become like the noonday. The Lord
will guide you always. . . . You
will be like a well-watered
garden, like a spring whose
waters never fail."

Isaiah 58:6–7, 9–11

Jesus, be in my fast . . .

Moses: "Do Not Commit Adultery"
Exodus 20:14

Jesus, be in my marriage . . .

Marriage is compared to Jesus' love for the Church,
His Body. It is natural for a woman to be attracted to
many men, whether to spirit, mind or body. To resist
temptation I need to be covered with
the spiritual armor of God daily. The
belt of truth is also chastity, fidelity
to the promise I made my husband.
In prayer I can see each creature
as made in God's image, designed to be a praise, a light,
a pure vessel.

Father God, Lover of all of
me, I give You my mar-
riage, my sexuality, my
relationships with every
other person—male/female,
fleeting/intense. Jesus, be in
my marriage . . .

Marriage should be honored by all, and
the marriage bed kept pure, for God
will judge the adulterer and all the
sexually immoral.   Hebrews 13:4

Jesus: "It Is Finished"
John 19:30

Jesus, be in my weakness . . .

"I do nothing on my own," Jesus said, ". . . I always do what pleases him" (John 8:28–29). Though Jesus was the King of kings, He often chose the route of weakness. Certainly on the cross, dying, He embraced weakness; He refused to work a miracle and save Himself. Failure to act because I am obeying God may seem like weakness to those who urge me to use my strength in another direction.

Father God, Creator of the universe, when I have done all I can, and my weakness seems like failure, I trust that Your will will be done in spite of me. Jesus, be in my weakness . . .

But he said to me, "My grace is sufficient for you, for my power is made perfect in weakness."
2 Corinthians 12:9

Moses: "Do Not Lie"
Exodus 20:16

Jesus, be in my sincerity . . .

The heart is deceptive, the Bible says,
and I know that from experience.
Openness and guilelessness are not
natural qualities. I cannot see the depth
of my own hypocrisy. As I expose myself to
the light that burns away everything not of
Him, the "me" that is left is the shining
image of God I was created to be. I cannot
see that light in myself, but
others are warmed by it.

Father God of Light, perfect
Truth, I want to be open before
You and free from deceptions.
Jesus, be in my sincerity . . .

Let us draw near to God with a sin-
cere heart in full assurance of faith,
having our hearts sprinkled to cleanse
us from a guilty conscience.
                    Hebrews 10:22

Jesus: Committed His Spirit
Luke 23:46

Jesus, be in my releasing . . .

Yesterday I visited my daddy who is dying of cancer in
the hospital. Though his mind was not with us, he
kept saying, "Let's go." Each one in that room had
releasing to do. In order to learn to walk, the child
must let go of the hand of the caring parent and take
those first steps alone. The parent also must release
the child. So it is in the presence of death. The Spirit
of Jesus, the undiluted love and light of God is waiting, actively urging us to
come, cross over, enter into
that place prepared. To release; to set free; to let go;
to set free from pain and
cares—this is deliverance
and liberation.

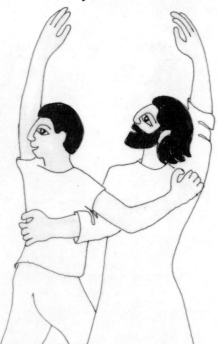

Loving Father God, into
Your hands I commit my
spirit and the lives of those
I love. Jesus, be in my
releasing . . .

What a wretched man I am! Who
will rescue me from this body of
death? Thanks be to God—
through Jesus Christ our Lord!
Romans 7:24–25

Moses: "Do Not Covet"
Exodus 20:17

Jesus, be in my simplicity

Simplicity is the opposite of covet-
ousness. Simplicity is centered in,
pared down to basics, undivided,
unpretentious, uncomplicated. To
simplify my life in this age is not
easy but necessary. Jesus had His
eyes singlemindedly on what
pleased the heavenly Father. He
approached death with the same
simplicity and was victorious over
it. The promise is mine as well.

Thank You, Father God, that You are
One God in all, through all, filling all.
In You I can find all that I need. Jesus,
be in my simplicity . . .

Now this is our boast: Our conscience testifies
that we have conducted ourselves in the world,
and especially in our relations with you, in the
holiness and sincerity that are from God.
                                    2 Corinthians 1:12

Jesus: "Peace Be With You"
John 20:19–20

Jesus, be in my glorifying . . .

Easter joy! The sorrow, the pain, the tears of cross
and grave were not forgotten but transfigured with
glorious light. The guilt and shame at failures were
forgiven by Jesus' words as He entered that locked
upper room. Jesus still enters into the sealed rooms of
my heart, and into my relationships, assuring me of
His full acceptance and His complete victory over the
powers of death and this world. In Him
I am an overcomer.

Father God, as my soul
rejoices in Jesus' resurrection reality, I know You
have taken my daddy into
that place undimmed by
tears where Your glory
shines. Jesus, be in
my glorifying . . .

But even if I am being poured
out like a drink offering on
the sacrifice and service coming from your faith, I am glad
and rejoice with all of you.
So you too should be glad
and rejoice with me.
Philippians 2:17–18

Moses: Sang to God
Exodus 15:2

Jesus, be in my gladness . . .

Through the valley of the shadow of death, through
the pain, rejections, fear and grief, the light glows today with new beauty. The light of the empty cross, the
open tomb, shines stronger now than ever because of
my daddy and the millions of saints who have gone
before. They rejoice with myriad angels in the heavens
and are preparing a new earth.

Father God, though I glimpse Your glory I must complete my mission here—but this Easter it is with more
glad confidence and urgency than ever before. Jesus, be
in my gladness . . .

Shout for joy to the Lord, all the earth. Serve the Lord with gladness; come before him with joyful songs. Know that the Lord is
God. It is he who made us, and we are his.   Psalm 100:1–3